GUIDED BY TAROT

2024

WEEKLY PLANNER

JULY 2023–DECEMBER 2024

ROCK
POINT

2024 YEAR AT A GLANCE

JANUARY

S	M	T	W	T	F	S
	1	2	3	4	5	6
7	8	9	10	11	12	13
14	15	16	17	18	19	20
21	22	23	24	25	26	27
28	29	30	31			

FEBRUARY

S	M	T	W	T	F	S
				1	2	3
4	5	6	7	8	9	10
11	12	13	14	15	16	17
18	19	20	21	22	23	24
25	26	27	28	29		

MARCH

S	M	T	W	T	F	S
					1	2
3	4	5	6	7	8	9
10	11	12	13	14	15	16
17	18	19	20	21	22	23
24	25	26	27	28	29	30
31						

APRIL

S	M	T	W	T	F	S
	1	2	3	4	5	6
7	8	9	10	11	12	13
14	15	16	17	18	19	20
21	22	23	24	25	26	27
28	29	30				

MAY

S	M	T	W	T	F	S
			1	2	3	4
5	6	7	8	9	10	11
12	13	14	15	16	17	18
19	20	21	22	23	24	25
26	27	28	29	30	31	

JUNE

S	M	T	W	T	F	S
						1
2	3	4	5	6	7	8
9	10	11	12	13	14	15
16	17	18	19	20	21	22
23	24	25	26	27	28	29
30						

JULY

S	M	T	W	T	F	S
	1	2	3	4	5	6
7	8	9	10	11	12	13
14	15	16	17	18	19	20
21	22	23	24	25	26	27
28	29	30	31			

AUGUST

S	M	T	W	T	F	S
				1	2	3
4	5	6	7	8	9	10
11	12	13	14	15	16	17
18	19	20	21	22	23	24
25	26	27	28	29	30	31

SEPTEMBER

S	M	T	W	T	F	S
1	2	3	4	5	6	7
8	9	10	11	12	13	14
15	16	17	18	19	20	21
22	23	24	25	26	27	28
29	30					

OCTOBER

S	M	T	W	T	F	S
		1	2	3	4	5
6	7	8	9	10	11	12
13	14	15	16	17	18	19
20	21	22	23	24	25	26
27	28	29	30	31		

NOVEMBER

S	M	T	W	T	F	S
					1	2
3	4	5	6	7	8	9
10	11	12	13	14	15	16
17	18	19	20	21	22	23
24	25	26	27	28	29	30

DECEMBER

S	M	T	W	T	F	S
1	2	3	4	5	6	7
8	9	10	11	12	13	14
15	16	17	18	19	20	21
22	23	24	25	26	27	28
29	30	31				

2025 YEAR AT A GLANCE

JANUARY

S	M	T	W	T	F	S
			1	2	3	4
5	6	7	8	9	10	11
12	13	14	15	16	17	18
19	20	21	22	23	24	25
26	27	28	29	30	31	

FEBRUARY

S	M	T	W	T	F	S
						1
2	3	4	5	6	7	8
9	10	11	12	13	14	15
16	17	18	19	20	21	22
23	24	25	26	27	28	

MARCH

S	M	T	W	T	F	S
						1
2	3	4	5	6	7	8
9	10	11	12	13	14	15
16	17	18	19	20	21	22
23	24	25	26	27	28	29
30	31					

APRIL

S	M	T	W	T	F	S
		1	2	3	4	5
6	7	8	9	10	11	12
13	14	15	16	17	18	19
20	21	22	23	24	25	26
27	28	29	30			

MAY

S	M	T	W	T	F	S
				1	2	3
4	5	6	7	8	9	10
11	12	13	14	15	16	17
18	19	20	21	22	23	24
25	26	27	28	29	30	31

JUNE

S	M	T	W	T	F	S
1	2	3	4	5	6	7
8	9	10	11	12	13	14
15	16	17	18	19	20	21
22	23	24	25	26	27	28
29	30					

JULY

S	M	T	W	T	F	S
		1	2	3	4	5
6	7	8	9	10	11	12
13	14	15	16	17	18	19
20	21	22	23	24	25	26
27	28	29	30	31		

AUGUST

S	M	T	W	T	F	S
					1	2
3	4	5	6	7	8	9
10	11	12	13	14	15	16
17	18	19	20	21	22	23
24	25	26	27	28	29	30
31						

SEPTEMBER

S	M	T	W	T	F	S
	1	2	3	4	5	6
7	8	9	10	11	12	13
14	15	16	17	18	19	20
21	22	23	24	25	26	27
28	29	30				

OCTOBER

S	M	T	W	T	F	S
			1	2	3	4
5	6	7	8	9	10	11
12	13	14	15	16	17	18
19	20	21	22	23	24	25
26	27	28	29	30	31	

NOVEMBER

S	M	T	W	T	F	S
						1
2	3	4	5	6	7	8
9	10	11	12	13	14	15
16	17	18	19	20	21	22
23	24	25	26	27	28	29
30						

DECEMBER

S	M	T	W	T	F	S
	1	2	3	4	5	6
7	8	9	10	11	12	13
14	15	16	17	18	19	20
21	22	23	24	25	26	27
28	29	30	31			

MONTHLY
FEATURED CARD

You've given yourself a magical gift by choosing to let your intuition and the tarot guide you through these next 18 months. There are countless benefits of reading tarot cards, but gaining insight into how you can make the most of your year, and grow spiritually while you're at it, is one of the most self-loving and effective.

To receive clear messages from the cards, they must be cleansed to rid them of any lingering energies before each use. One of the most effective methods is to choose a cleansing incense and pass the cards through the smoke. Another way is to leave them on a windowsill for 24 hours where they can bask in the light of the moon and the sun. Or you can store them in a box or a bag with a clear quartz crystal.

MONTHLY THREE-CARD SPREAD

Each month opens with a featured card to support your reading and a three-card spread that will help you to begin your month with a positive and focused outlook. To do this, shuffle the cards until your intuition signals you to stop. From the top of the pile, draw three cards and lay them alongside each other in a horizontal line. The first card reveals your goals for that month. The second card will show the obstacle or challenge you will face. And the third card represents the action you can take or the perspective you should lean into.

Your reading is then followed up by some focused questions for you to think about as you proceed through your month. At the end of each weekly page, you'll find summaries of card meanings and tarot reading tips. Practice your monthly readings by pulling three cards for July, then see what messages the cards have for you this month. Talk to the cards, ask them questions, dig deep into the answers you receive and how they can improve your life and mindset.

JULY 2023

NOTES	SUNDAY	MONDAY	TUESDAY
	2 ○	3	4
			INDEPENDENCE DAY (US)
	9 ☽	10	11
	16 ●	17	18
	23	24 ☾	25
	30	31	

JULY 2023

WEDNESDAY	THURSDAY	FRIDAY	SATURDAY
			1 CANADA DAY (CAN)
5	6	7	8
12	13	14	15
19	20	21	22
26	27	28	29

DEATH

When first learning tarot, many people are afraid of drawing the Death card. But fear not! Far from a bad omen, this is a card of new beginnings. Something is coming to an end and you're about to begin a new, exciting chapter. This card signals rebirth, renewal, and getting out of old habits. When you draw this card, be courageous! Embrace change and thrive.

MONDAY (JUNE)

26

TUESDAY (JUNE)

27

WEDNESDAY (JUNE)

28

THURSDAY (JUNE)

29

FRIDAY (JUNE)

30

SATURDAY CANADA DAY (CAN)

1

SUNDAY

2

JULY 2023

MONDAY ○

3

TUESDAY INDEPENDENCE DAY (US)

4

WEDNESDAY

5

THURSDAY

6

FRIDAY

7

SATURDAY

8

SUNDAY

9

QUEEN OF SWORDS

What you have learned and gone
through has given you wisdom, as well as
independence and a strong set of principles.

JULY 2023

MONDAY ◗   10

TUESDAY   11

WEDNESDAY   12

THURSDAY   13

FRIDAY

14

SATURDAY

15

SUNDAY

16

PAGE OF WANDS

Be open to that which is new and exciting. Set
out on an adventure. Be courageously yourself.
Explore. Be brave! It is all part of the process
of renewal.

JULY 2023

MONDAY ● 17

TUESDAY 18

WEDNESDAY 19

THURSDAY 20

FRIDAY

21

SATURDAY

22

SUNDAY

23

NINE OF CUPS

Satisfaction is its own reward. Take stock
of life and love. Find pleasure in what you
have achieved. Indulge yourself. Relish
what life has to offer you.

JULY 2023

MONDAY

24

TUESDAY ☽

25

WEDNESDAY

26

THURSDAY

27

FRIDAY

28

SATURDAY

29

SUNDAY

30

TAROT TIP

Before you do a reading, clear your mind with
a short meditation so that you can hear your
intuition clearly.

AUGUST

STRENGTH

STRENGTH

The focus of August is strength of character. There is confidence in strength, a feeling of permanence and solidity. This is a card of determination, but also of thoughtfulness and compassion for others. You have strength. You have determination in your convictions. You see others through a lens of kindness.

LAY OUT A THREE-CARD SPREAD AND ASK THE CARDS

GOAL   OBSTACLE   ACTION

1. What goal do I need to focus on this month?

....

2. What obstacle or challenge will I face this month?

....

3. In what ways can I lean on my own inner strength to make this a successful month?

....

AUGUST 2023

NOTES	SUNDAY	MONDAY	TUESDAY
			○ 1
	6	7 ◗	8
		SUMMER BANK HOLIDAY (UK-SCT)	
	13	14	15
	20	21	22
	27	28	29
		SUMMER BANK HOLIDAY (UK-ENG / NIR / WAL)	

AUGUST 2023

WEDNESDAY	THURSDAY	FRIDAY	SATURDAY
2	3	4	5
9	10	11	12
● 16	17	18	19
23 ◗	24	25	26
○ 30	31		

TWO

OF CUPS

Two can be stronger than one. Harmony and partnership trumps disunity. A romance could be waiting, or a new friendship. They might be coming to you, or you could have to go looking. Keep your eyes and heart open.

JULY/AUGUST

MONDAY (JULY)   31

TUESDAY ◯   1

WEDNESDAY   2

THURSDAY   3

FRIDAY   4

SATURDAY   5

SUNDAY   6

AUGUST 2023

MONDAY SUMMER BANK HOLIDAY (UK-SCT)

7

TUESDAY ☽

8

WEDNESDAY

9

THURSDAY

10

FRIDAY

11

SATURDAY

12

SUNDAY

13

JUSTICE

Everything has its opposite. For every up,
there's a down, and for every injustice, there is
a righteous act. Justice is on its way to you.

AUGUST 2023

MONDAY 14

TUESDAY 15

WEDNESDAY ● 16

THURSDAY 17

FRIDAY 18

SATURDAY 19

SUNDAY 20

FIVE OF PENTACLES

Try as you might, not everything comes up
roses. When you hit a bad patch, remind
yourself that help can usually be found.
You just need to look around you.

AUGUST 2023

MONDAY 21

TUESDAY 22

WEDNESDAY 23

THURSDAY 24

FRIDAY   25

SATURDAY   26

SUNDAY   27

TAROT TIP

It's okay to keep your questions general if you
don't know what you need. It's always good
to have a category in mind though. Career?
Relationship? Goals?

SEPTEMBER

THE WORLD

THE
WORLD

You are surrounded by change. But now you can contemplate permanence, stability, and the cycles of life. Maybe you are fulfilled and accomplished. Perhaps you feel there is more to be done. Is this the end of a journey or just a beginning? Change doesn't have to be feared.

LAY OUT A THREE-CARD SPREAD AND ASK THE CARDS

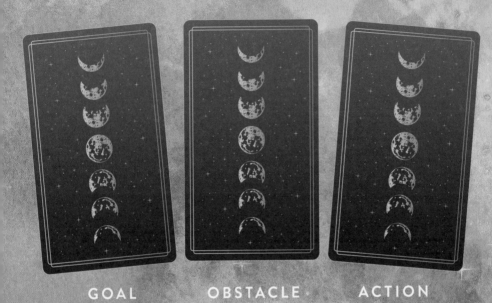

GOAL   OBSTACLE   ACTION

1. What goal do I need to focus on this month?

....

2. What obstacle or challenge will I face this month?

....

3. How can I nurture a sense of stability this month?

....

SEPTEMBER 2023

NOTES	SUNDAY	MONDAY	TUESDAY
	3	4	5
	FATHER'S DAY (AUS / NZ)	LABOR DAY (US) LABOUR DAY (CAN)	
	10	11	12
	GRANDPARENTS' DAY (US)	PATRIOT DAY (US)	
	17	18	19
	24	25	26
	YOM KIPPUR (BEGINS AT SUNDOWN)		

SEPTEMBER 2023

WEDNESDAY	THURSDAY	FRIDAY	SATURDAY
		1	2
☽ 6	7	8	9
13 ●	14	15 **ROSH HASHANAH (BEGINS AT SUNDOWN)** **FIRST DAY OF NATIONAL HISPANIC HERITAGE MONTH**	16
20	21 ☾	22	23 **FALL EQUINOX**
27	28 ○	29 **SUKKOT (BEGINS AT SUNDOWN)**	30

NINE

OF SWORDS

There is no limit to things that you can be worried about. Some can be real, but others may be just phantoms, anxieties, or figments of your imagination. Separate the real from the imagined. Seek your inner truth.

AUGUST/SEPTEMBER

MONDAY (AUGUST) SUMMER BANK HOLIDAY (UK-ENG / NIR / WAL)

28

TUESDAY (AUGUST)

29

WEDNESDAY (AUGUST) ○

30

THURSDAY (AUGUST)

31

FRIDAY

1

SATURDAY

2

SUNDAY FATHER'S DAY (AUS / NZ)

3

SEPTEMBER 2023

MONDAY LABOR DAY (US) / LABOUR DAY (CAN)

4

TUESDAY

5

WEDNESDAY ◗

6

THURSDAY

7

FRIDAY

8

. . . .

SATURDAY

9

. . . .

SUNDAY GRANDPARENTS' DAY (US)

10

. . . .

TWO OF WANDS

Make plans for the next step of your journey.
You may have to decide between sticking with
what you know and breaking with the past.

SEPTEMBER 2023

MONDAY PATRIOT DAY (US)

11

TUESDAY

12

WEDNESDAY

13

THURSDAY ●

14

FRIDAY ROSH HASHANAH (BEGINS AT SUNDOWN) /
FIRST DAY OF NATIONAL HISPANIC HERITAGE MONTH

15

SATURDAY

16

SUNDAY

17

KNIGHT OF CUPS

New possibilities could be headed your way:
romance, adventure, or some long-desired
opportunity. Be relaxed but prepared.

SEPTEMBER 2023

MONDAY

18

TUESDAY

19

WEDNESDAY

20

THURSDAY

21

FRIDAY ◖

22

SATURDAY FALL EQUINOX

23

SUNDAY YOM KIPPUR (BEGINS AT SUNDOWN)

24

TAROT TIP
Have a specific question in the forefront of
your mind while you shuffle your cards to
infuse that energy into them.

OCTOBER

THE TOWER

THE TOWER

Sudden disruption may be on the way, whether you are aware of it or not. You could have built a foundation on assumptions that are shakier than you knew. What kind of upheavals have you had recently? How did you bounce back? Draw on that strength to face the change that is coming without fear or hesitation.

LAY OUT A THREE-CARD SPREAD AND ASK THE CARDS

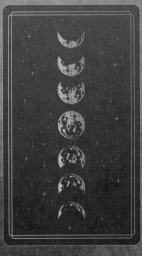

GOAL   **OBSTACLE**   **ACTION**

1. What goal do I need to focus on this month?

2. What obstacle or challenge will I face this month?

3. How can I draw on my strength to see things in a new light?

OCTOBER 2023

NOTES	SUNDAY	MONDAY	TUESDAY
		1	2 LABOUR DAY (AUS-ACT / NSW / SA)	3
	8	9 INDIGENOUS PEOPLES' DAY (US) / COLUMBUS DAY (US) / THANKSGIVING DAY (CAN)	10
	15	16	17
	22	23 LABOUR DAY (NZ)	24
	29	30	31 HALLOWEEN

OCTOBER 2023

WEDNESDAY	THURSDAY	FRIDAY	SATURDAY
4	5 ◗	6	7
			SIMCHAT TORAH (BEGINS AT SUNDOWN)
11	12	13	14 ●
18	19	20 ◖	21
25	26	27 ○	28

SEVEN

OF PENTACLES

Pausing, in work or in your journey, gives you an opportunity for rest. It can also provide a chance for reassessment. What are you laboring for, after all? Are you headed in the right direction? Maybe it is time to check that map. It's ok to do nothing.

SEPTEMBER/OCTOBER

MONDAY (SEPTEMBER)   25

TUESDAY (SEPTEMBER)   26

WEDNESDAY (SEPTEMBER)   27

THURSDAY (SEPTEMBER)   28

FRIDAY (SEPTEMBER) SUKKOT (BEGINS AT SUNDOWN) ○   29

SATURDAY (SEPTEMBER)   30

SUNDAY   1

OCTOBER 2023

MONDAY LABOUR DAY (AUS-ACT / NSW / SA)

2

TUESDAY

3

WEDNESDAY

4

THURSDAY

5

FRIDAY ◗

6

SATURDAY SIMCHAT TORAH (BEGINS AT SUNDOWN)

7

SUNDAY

8

THREE OF PENTACLES

You have talents. But not everything you have
was secured on your own. You've had help
along the way. Practice gratitude.

OCTOBER 2023

MONDAY INDIGENOUS PEOPLES' DAY (US) / COLUMBUS DAY (US) / THANKSGIVING DAY (CAN)

9

TUESDAY

10

WEDNESDAY

11

THURSDAY

12

FRIDAY 13

SATURDAY ● 14

SUNDAY 15

TEN OF SWORDS

Things may look dark. When dealt a serious
blow, it can be easy to lose hope. But you are
still standing. Now is a time for rebuilding.

OCTOBER 2023

MONDAY

16

TUESDAY

17

WEDNESDAY

18

THURSDAY

19

FRIDAY

20

SATURDAY

21

SUNDAY

22

PAGE OF CUPS

Inspiration is like lightning, only not as
dangerous (usually). It cannot be planned, it
makes your hair stand up, and afterward you
might look at things differently.

OCTOBER 2023

MONDAY LABOUR DAY (NZ)

23

TUESDAY

24

WEDNESDAY

25

THURSDAY

26

FRIDAY

27

SATURDAY ◯

28

SUNDAY

29

TAROT TIP

Do a reading before any major event to help
give you insight. This works really well for a job
interview or a date!

NOVEMBER

THE SUN

THE
SUN

Some card meanings are just less equivocal than others. This one? It's fantastic. Happiness, hope, new beginnings—and that's just the start of it! There is innocence here, along with the restoration that comes after trials and tribulations. Think of renewal, strength, and the source of your joy. Imagine all that you will be able to accomplish. Manifest your desires.

LAY OUT A THREE-CARD SPREAD AND ASK THE CARDS

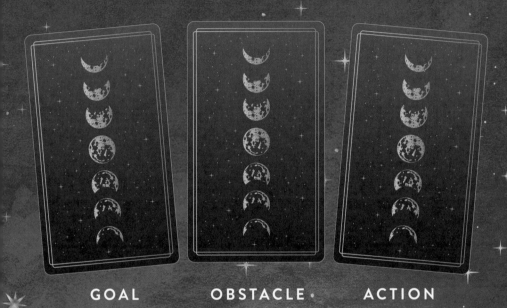

GOAL   OBSTACLE   ACTION

1. What goal do I need to focus on this month?

2. What obstacle or challenge will I face this month?

3. In what ways can I express my gratitude for all I have and the beauty in my life?

NOVEMBER 2023

NOTES	SUNDAY	MONDAY	TUESDAY
	◗ 5	6	7
			ELECTION DAY (US)
	12 ●	13	14
	FIRST DAY OF DIWALI		
	19 ◖	20	21
	26 ○	27	28

NOVEMBER 2023

WEDNESDAY	THURSDAY	FRIDAY	SATURDAY
1 ALL SAINTS' DAY	2	3	4
8	9	10	11 VETERANS DAY (US)
15	16	17	18
22	23 THANKSGIVING DAY (US)	24 NATIVE AMERICAN HERITAGE DAY (US)	25
29	30		

THREE

OF WANDS

You have been successful. Not everything has been taken care of, there are still more challenges to come. But you are in a position of power and confidence. You have good visibility for what is to come. There is also the potential of finding a partner who can help you achieve the kind of success that you have long dreamed of. Bask in what you have accomplished, your reward is great.

OCTOBER/NOVEMBER

MONDAY (OCTOBER)

30

TUESDAY (OCTOBER) HALLOWEEN

31

WEDNESDAY ALL SAINTS' DAY

1

THURSDAY

2

FRIDAY

3

SATURDAY

4

SUNDAY)

5

NOVEMBER 2023

MONDAY

6

TUESDAY ELECTION DAY (US)

7

WEDNESDAY

8

THURSDAY

9

FRIDAY 10

SATURDAY VETERANS DAY (US) 11

SUNDAY FIRST DAY OF DIWALI 12

FIVE OF CUPS

You've lost something of importance or faced
a trying time. But keeping your head down
makes it hard to see the good that is coming.
Look life right in the eye.

NOVEMBER 2023

MONDAY ● 13

TUESDAY 14

WEDNESDAY 15

THURSDAY 16

FRIDAY

17

SATURDAY

18

SUNDAY

19

EIGHT OF WANDS

Things within you and your life are in motion. Take
hold of that energy and use it to your advantage
by making positive changes to bad habits.

NOVEMBER 2023

MONDAY 🌓

20

TUESDAY

21

WEDNESDAY

22

THURSDAY THANKSGIVING DAY (US)

23

FRIDAY NATIVE AMERICAN HERITAGE DAY (US)

24

SATURDAY

25

SUNDAY

26

TAROT TIP

It's good to reset your deck every so often.
Place your deck in its original order starting with
the Fool card, making sure that all cards are
right side up. Then, cleanse and shuffle them.

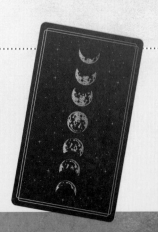

DECEMBER

WHEEL OF FORTUNE

WHEEL
OF FORTUNE

Sometimes everything is a gamble. That may not be your preference; not everybody likes to leave things hanging on a spin of the wheel. Or maybe you find the game of chance exciting. Either way, change is coming. Spin that wheel like you mean it. You are the house, and the house always wins.

LAY OUT A THREE-CARD SPREAD AND ASK THE CARDS

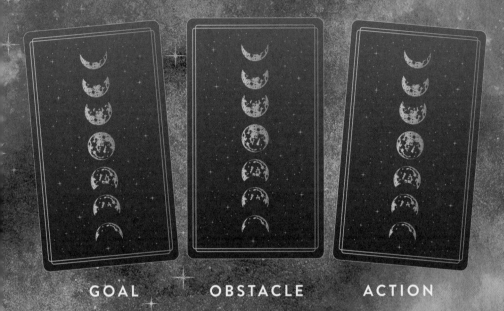

GOAL   OBSTACLE   ACTION

1. What goal do I need to focus on this month?

....

....

2. What obstacle or challenge will I face this month?

....

....

3. In what ways can I make the most of the changes that are coming in my life?

....

....

DECEMBER 2023

NOTES	SUNDAY	MONDAY	TUESDAY
	3	4 ◗	5
	INTERNATIONAL DAY OF PERSONS WITH DISABILITIES		
	10	11 ●	12
	HUMAN RIGHTS DAY		
	17	18 ◖	19
	24	25 ○	26
	CHRISTMAS EVE		BOXING DAY (UK / CAN / AUS / NZ)
	31		
	NEW YEAR'S EVE	CHRISTMAS DAY	FIRST DAY OF KWANZAA

DECEMBER 2023

WEDNESDAY	THURSDAY	FRIDAY	SATURDAY
		1 WORLD AIDS DAY	2
6	7 HANUKKAH (BEGINS AT SUNDOWN)	8	9
13	14	15	16
20	21 WINTER SOLSTICE	22	23
27	28	29	30

SIX

OF PENTACLES

Have you come into some good fortune? If so, spread the wealth! Nothing shows your appreciation for everything you have been given like paying it forward. Express gratitude and share.

NOVEMBER/DECEMBER

MONDAY (NOVEMBER) ○

27

TUESDAY (NOVEMBER)

28

WEDNESDAY (NOVEMBER)

29

THURSDAY (NOVEMBER)

30

FRIDAY WORLD AIDS DAY

1

SATURDAY

2

SUNDAY INTERNATIONAL DAY OF PERSONS WITH DISABILITIES

3

DECEMBER 2023

MONDAY 4

TUESDAY ☽ 5

WEDNESDAY 6

THURSDAY HANUKKAH (BEGINS AT SUNDOWN) 7

FRIDAY

8

SATURDAY

9

SUNDAY HUMAN RIGHTS DAY

10

SIX OF SWORDS

Transitions are necessary, but they can often be difficult. This is a good time to let go of the burdens of your past. Face the future clearly, honestly, and positively.

DECEMBER 2023

MONDAY

11

TUESDAY ●

12

WEDNESDAY

13

THURSDAY

14

FRIDAY 15

SATURDAY 16

SUNDAY 17

QUEEN OF CUPS

Intuition and empathy are your guides. Listen to your inner voice and lean into its advice.

DECEMBER 2023

MONDAY 18

TUESDAY ◐ 19

WEDNESDAY 20

THURSDAY WINTER SOLSTICE 21

FRIDAY

22

SATURDAY

23

SUNDAY CHRISTMAS EVE

24

PAGE OF SWORDS

Focus and direction may not be your strong
suits at the moment. New ideas, possibilities,
dreams, and desires keep your head buzzing.
Harness that flow and manifest.

DECEMBER 2023

MONDAY CHRISTMAS DAY

25

TUESDAY BOXING DAY (UK / CAN / AUS / NZ) / FIRST DAY OF KWANZAA ◯

26

WEDNESDAY

27

THURSDAY

28

FRIDAY

29

SATURDAY

30

SUNDAY NEW YEAR'S EVE

31

TAROT TIP

Don't be afraid when you pull a reversed
card. These are great for showing you
ways you can grow.

JANUARY

TEMPERANCE

TEMPERANCE

There is a time to commit yourself fully and a time to hang back. Where have you been putting your time and energy? Sometimes we can go too far without realizing it. Now is a time to consider whether there is imbalance in your life and if so, how you can restore order. Remember, you are in this for the long haul!

LAY OUT A THREE-CARD SPREAD AND ASK THE CARDS

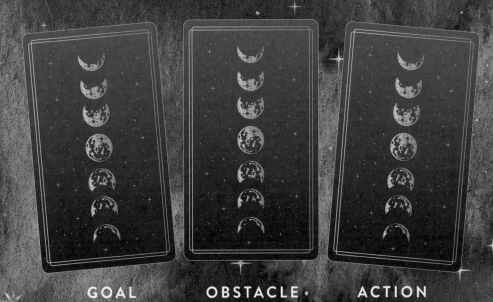

GOAL   OBSTACLE   ACTION

1. What goal do I need to focus on this month?

....

2. What obstacle or challenge will I face this month?

....

3. In what ways can I restore balance to my life?

....

JANUARY 2024

NOTES	SUNDAY	MONDAY	TUESDAY
....		**1** NEW YEAR'S DAY	**2** NEW YEAR HOLIDAY (UK-SCT)
....	**7**	**8**	**9**
....	**14**	**15** CIVIL RIGHTS DAY (US) MARTIN LUTHER KING JR. DAY (US)	**16**
....	**21**	**22**	**23**
....	**28**	**29**	**30**

JANUARY 2024

WEDNESDAY	THURSDAY	FRIDAY	SATURDAY
◐ 3	4	5	6
10 ●	11	12	13
◖ 17	18	19	20
24 ○	25	26 AUSTRALIA DAY (AUS)	27 HOLOCAUST REMEMBRANCE DAY
31			

SIX

OF CUPS

The past is in the past, but it never disappears. Are you returning to a familiar place with strong associations? Is there a memory you cannot shake? There might be a sensation, a discovery, or even a person from earlier in your life worth revisiting. The past is a gentle teacher.

JANUARY

MONDAY NEW YEAR'S DAY

1

TUESDAY NEW YEAR HOLIDAY (UK-SCT)

2

WEDNESDAY ☽

3

THURSDAY

4

FRIDAY

5

SATURDAY

6

SUNDAY

7

JANUARY 2024

MONDAY

8

TUESDAY

9

WEDNESDAY

10

THURSDAY ●

11

FRIDAY

12

SATURDAY

13

SUNDAY

14

THE HANGED MAN

Sometimes things look worse than
they are. It could be time to look at
everything from a newer, fresher angle.
Reconsider old assumptions.

JANUARY 2024

MONDAY CIVIL RIGHTS DAY (US) / MARTIN LUTHER KING JR. DAY (US)

15

TUESDAY

16

WEDNESDAY ◖

17

THURSDAY

18

FRIDAY

19

SATURDAY

20

SUNDAY

21

EIGHT OF SWORDS

Some traps we set ourselves. You're holding yourself back and now's the time to be vigilant. Seek out what's blocking you and unset the trap.

JANUARY 2024

MONDAY   22

TUESDAY   23

WEDNESDAY   24

THURSDAY ○   25

FRIDAY AUSTRALIA DAY (AUS)

26

SATURDAY HOLOCAUST REMEMBRANCE DAY

27

SUNDAY

28

TAROT TIP

Question to ask your tarot: I feel stuck. What can I do to start a new path in life?
Question not to ask your tarot: Money would be great. Am I going to win the lottery?

FEBRUARY

THE STAR

THE
STAR

Hope and regeneration are always within reach. We all make mistakes or poor decisions from time to time which can make us feel low and unworthy. Give yourself a break, you're only human, after all. Reaffirm the greatness within you. Have faith in yourself and your inner resilience. Burn bright because the world needs your unique light.

LAY OUT A THREE-CARD SPREAD AND ASK THE CARDS

GOAL   OBSTACLE   ACTION

1. What goal do I need to focus on this month?

....

2. What obstacle or challenge will I face this month?

....

3. In what ways can I be more resilient and believe in myself during challenges?

....

FEBRUARY 2024

NOTES	SUNDAY	MONDAY	TUESDAY
....			
....	4	5	6
			WAITANGI DAY OBSERVED (NZ)
....	11	12	13
....	18	19	20
			PRESIDENTS' DAY (US)
....	25	26	27

FEBRUARY 2024

WEDNESDAY	THURSDAY	FRIDAY	SATURDAY
	1 ◐	2	3
	FIRST DAY OF BLACK HISTORY MONTH	GROUNDHOG DAY (US / CAN)	
7	8 ●	9	10
			CHINESE NEW YEAR
14	15 ◑	16	17
VALENTINE'S DAY ASH WEDNESDAY			
21	22	23 ○	24
28			

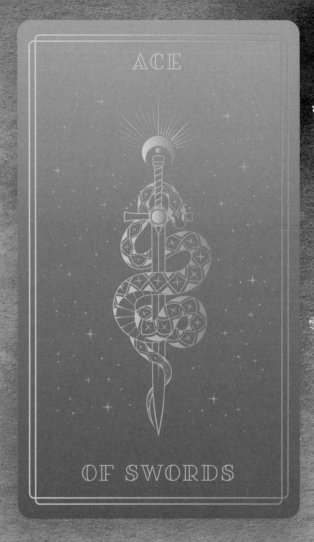

ACE

OF SWORDS

Breakthrough, clarity, truth, new ideas, new opportunity, and perspective are in abundance. When life is going well (or not) we can get into a rut with our thinking. A breakthrough is on its way to you. New ideas, clarity, and truth are working to manifest in your life. Eureka!

JANUARY/FEBRUARY

MONDAY (JANUARY)

29

TUESDAY (JANUARY)

30

WEDNESDAY (JANUARY)

31

THURSDAY FIRST DAY OF BLACK HISTORY MONTH

1

FRIDAY GROUNDHOG DAY (US / CAN) ◗

2

SATURDAY

3

SUNDAY

4

FEBRUARY 2024

MONDAY 5

TUESDAY WAITANGI DAY OBSERVED (NZ) 6

WEDNESDAY 7

THURSDAY 8

FRIDAY ● 9

SATURDAY CHINESE NEW YEAR 10

SUNDAY 11

FIVE OF WANDS

Be aware of conflict and dissent in your life but
do not seek them out. These struggles can be
highly disruptive but can also be a source of
renewal. Look for lessons in the strife.

FEBRUARY 2024

MONDAY 12

TUESDAY 13

WEDNESDAY VALENTINE'S DAY / ASH WEDNESDAY 14

THURSDAY 15

FRIDAY ◖

16

SATURDAY

17

SUNDAY

18

NINE OF WANDS

Sometimes it seems as if it isn't one thing it's another. This card reminds you that despite adversity, your inner strength will get you through.

FEBRUARY 2024

MONDAY PRESIDENTS' DAY (US)

19

TUESDAY

20

WEDNESDAY

21

THURSDAY

22

FRIDAY

23

SATURDAY ◯

24

SUNDAY

25

TAROT TIP

Learn the meanings of the cards but try not to
be rigid. These are messages from the divine so
use your intuition to enlighten you.

MARCH

THE LOVERS

THE
LOVERS

There is reason for optimism and the potential for harmony. Things might be coming together that were long separated. You could be on the verge of overcoming an obstacle. There are connections to be made, and choices as well. Nurture your passions and do something creative to express yourself to others. Be open to new relationships.

LAY OUT A THREE-CARD SPREAD AND ASK THE CARDS

GOAL   OBSTACLE   ACTION

1. What goal do I need to focus on this month?

....

....

2. What obstacle or challenge will I face this month?

....

....

3. How can I learn from this challenge to help create harmony in my life?

....

....

MARCH 2024

NOTES	SUNDAY	MONDAY	TUESDAY
	◗ 3	4	5
	● 10	11	12
	RAMADAN (BEGINS AT SUNDOWN) MOTHERING SUNDAY (UK)	LABOUR DAY (AUS-VIC)	
	◖ 17	18	19
	ST. PATRICK'S DAY		SPRING EQUINOX
	24 ○	25	26
	PALM SUNDAY		
	31		
	EASTER		

MARCH 2024

WEDNESDAY	THURSDAY	FRIDAY	SATURDAY
		1	2
		FIRST DAY OF WOMEN'S HISTORY MONTH	
6	7	8	9
13	14	15	16
20	21	22	23
NOWRUZ			PURIM (BEGINS AT SUNDOWN)
27	28	29	30
		GOOD FRIDAY	

Only the lucky draw this card. Continue to work hard because what you're doing is sparking success and prosperity. This is a good time to follow your passions, embark on new ventures, take chances, put yourself out there, and try new things. You can't lose.

FEBRUARY/MARCH

MONDAY (FEBRUARY)

26

TUESDAY (FEBRUARY)

27

WEDNESDAY (FEBRUARY)

28

THURSDAY (FEBRUARY)

29

FRIDAY FIRST DAY OF WOMEN'S HISTORY MONTH

1

SATURDAY

2

SUNDAY ◗

3

MARCH 2024

MONDAY

4

TUESDAY

5

WEDNESDAY

6

THURSDAY

7

FRIDAY 8

SATURDAY 9

SUNDAY RAMADAN (BEGINS AT SUNDOWN) / MOTHERING SUNDAY (UK) ● 10

TWO OF PENTACLES

You have a lot going on. How are you balancing your priorities? Are you a good enough juggler or is it time to cut back?

MARCH 2024

MONDAY LABOUR DAY (AUS-VIC)

11

TUESDAY

12

WEDNESDAY

13

THURSDAY

14

FRIDAY 15

SATURDAY 16

SUNDAY ST. PATRICK'S DAY ◖ 17

FOUR OF PENTACLES

Once you have something you have long
desired, it is natural to want to keep it. But try
too hard and you might lose it. Protect what
you have. But do not forget to enjoy it as well.

MARCH 2024

MONDAY

18

TUESDAY SPRING EQUINOX

19

WEDNESDAY NOWRUZ

20

THURSDAY

21

FRIDAY 22

SATURDAY PURIM (BEGINS AT SUNDOWN) 23

SUNDAY PALM SUNDAY 24

KNIGHT OF WANDS

The unpredictability of life can bring
challenges. Focus and determination will
get you through. You have what it takes
to be a leader.

MARCH 2024

MONDAY ○   25

TUESDAY   26

WEDNESDAY   27

THURSDAY   28

FRIDAY GOOD FRIDAY

29

SATURDAY

30

SUNDAY EASTER

31

TAROT TIP

If you don't like your deck (maybe it was a gift),
look for one that has art that really speaks
to you. If you like what you see, you'll like
what you hear.

APRIL

THE FOOL

THE
FOOL

The world is full of risk and wonder and although situations will arise that you're unfamiliar with, the Universe is on your side. Maybe you feel embarrassed about your inexperience, or fear not knowing what to expect. Rather than cower, use this as a time to learn. Have faith in your future. You've got beginner's luck.

LAY OUT A THREE-CARD SPREAD AND ASK THE CARDS

GOAL   OBSTACLE   ACTION

1. What goal do I need to focus on this month?

....

....

2. What obstacle or challenge will I face this month?

....

....

3. In what ways can I stop doubting myself and learn from the unexpected?

....

....

APRIL 2024

NOTES	SUNDAY	MONDAY	TUESDAY
		☽ 1	2
		APRIL FOOLS' DAY	
	7 ●	8	9
			EID AL-FITR (BEGINS AT SUNDOWN)
	14	☾ 15	16
	21	22 ○	23
		PASSOVER (BEGINS AT SUNDOWN) EARTH DAY	
	28	29	30

APRIL 2024

WEDNESDAY	THURSDAY	FRIDAY	SATURDAY
3	4	5	6
10	11	12	13
17	18	19	20
24	25	26	27
ADMINISTRATIVE PROFESSIONALS' DAY (US)	ANZAC DAY (AUS / NZ)		

TEN

OF PENTACLES

It's time for a payout for all the hard work you've been putting into yourself, your outlook, your career, family, and finances. You're about to experience a windfall of wealth, whether that be physical or spiritual. This is also a time for family harmony, so share your prosperity with those you love. You may have faced some challenges, but this card asserts that it's all worth it in the end.

APRIL

MONDAY APRIL FOOLS' DAY

1

TUESDAY

2

WEDNESDAY

3

THURSDAY

4

FRIDAY

5

SATURDAY

6

SUNDAY

7

APRIL 2024

MONDAY ●

8

TUESDAY EID AL-FITR (BEGINS AT SUNDOWN)

9

WEDNESDAY

10

THURSDAY

11

FRIDAY

12

SATURDAY

13

SUNDAY

14

THREE OF CUPS

You are not alone. There are people in your life
to connect with—community, family, friends
new and old, maybe even an old enemy who
might have turned over a new leaf.

APRIL 2024

MONDAY ◗   15

TUESDAY   16

WEDNESDAY   17

THURSDAY   18

FRIDAY

19

SATURDAY

20

SUNDAY

21

ACE OF CUPS

This is a time of emotional abundance. New
relationships could be starting, or older ones
revitalized. Be inspired to make a fresh start.
Go with it!

APRIL 2024

MONDAY PASSOVER (BEGINS AT SUNDOWN) / EARTH DAY

22

TUESDAY ◯

23

WEDNESDAY ADMINISTRATIVE PROFESSIONALS' DAY (US)

24

THURSDAY ANZAC DAY (AUS / NZ)

25

FRIDAY

26

SATURDAY

27

SUNDAY

28

TAROT TIP

Try not to avoid or dread receiving any card in
the deck. Even the ones that might seem scary
at first carry messages that improve our lives.

MAY

THE EMPRESS

Your inner artist is ready to make an appearance. Anything you create can be considered art and now is your time to shine. Use your five senses to draw pleasure from your experiences and nurture the joy you feel. The feminine energy of sensuality, beauty, and creativity are manifesting for all genders, making this a great moment to start a new hobby or spend time with your partner.

LAY OUT A THREE-CARD SPREAD AND ASK THE CARDS

GOAL   OBSTACLE   ACTION

1. What goal do I need to focus on this month?

....

2. What obstacle or challenge will I face this month?

....

3. How can I overcome the fear of judgment and be myself?

....

MAY 2024

NOTES	SUNDAY	MONDAY	TUESDAY
	5	6 ●	7
	CINCO DE MAYO ORTHODOX EASTER	LABOUR DAY (AUS-QLD) EARLY MAY BANK HOLIDAY (UK)	
	12	13	14
	MOTHER'S DAY (US / CAN)		
	19	20	21
		VICTORIA DAY (CAN)	
	26	27	28
		SPRING BANK HOLIDAY (UK) MEMORIAL DAY (US)	

MAY 2024

WEDNESDAY	THURSDAY	FRIDAY	SATURDAY
☾ 1 FIRST DAY OF ASIAN AMERICAN AND PACIFIC ISLANDER HERITAGE MONTH	2	3	4 YOM HASHOAH (BEGINS AT SUNDOWN)
8	9	10	11
☾ 15	16	17	18
22 ○	23	24	25
29 ☾	30	31	

KING

OF CUPS

Maintain your balance. Rise above squabbles and negativity. Do not inhibit your feelings but direct them. Other people respect your even-handedness and wisdom. They will want your advice. But offer it carefully, as you can lead others astray if you're off balance.

APRIL/MAY

MONDAY (APRIL)　29

TUESDAY (APRIL)　30

WEDNESDAY　FIRST DAY OF ASIAN AMERICAN AND PACIFIC ISLANDER HERITAGE MONTH　1

THURSDAY　2

FRIDAY　3

SATURDAY　YOM HASHOAH (BEGINS AT SUNDOWN)　4

SUNDAY　CINCO DE MAYO / ORTHODOX EASTER　5

MAY 2024

MONDAY LABOUR DAY (AUS-QLD) / EARLY MAY BANK HOLIDAY (UK)

6

TUESDAY ●

7

WEDNESDAY

8

THURSDAY

9

FRIDAY

10

SATURDAY

11

SUNDAY MOTHER'S DAY (US / CAN)

12

TWO OF SWORDS

There are tough choices ahead of you. Keep
yourself balanced so that you can face
these challenges.

MAY 2024

MONDAY

13

TUESDAY

14

WEDNESDAY ☽

15

THURSDAY

16

FRIDAY

17

SATURDAY

18

SUNDAY

19

SEVEN OF SWORDS

You are likely trying to get away with
something. It may pass off without a hitch, but
if you're found out you'll face embarrassment
for being sneaky.

MAY 2024

MONDAY VICTORIA DAY (CAN)

20

TUESDAY

21

WEDNESDAY

22

THURSDAY ◯

23

FRIDAY

24

SATURDAY

25

SUNDAY

26

TAROT TIP

Establish a special place to keep your cards.
Whether it be a bag or a box, a drawer or a
shelf, this space can cleanse your deck and
infuse it with your energy.

JUNE

THE MAGICIAN

THE
MAGICIAN

Keep your feet on the earth and your eyes in the sky. Ground yourself but watch for what is coming. Is it time to open yourself to possibilities? Do you have untapped potential? Something previously hidden could be coming to light. The veil is lifting from the mirror.

LAY OUT A THREE-CARD SPREAD AND ASK THE CARDS

GOAL   OBSTACLE ·   ACTION

1. What goal do I need to focus on this month?

2. What obstacle or challenge will I face this month?

3. In what ways can I recognize and utilize my untapped potential?

JUNE 2024

	2	3	4
	9	10	11
	16	17	18
	FATHER'S DAY **(US / CAN / UK)**		
	23	24	25
	30		

JUNE 2024

WEDNESDAY	THURSDAY	FRIDAY	SATURDAY
			1 **FIRST DAY OF PRIDE MONTH**
5 ●	6	7	8
12	13	14 **FLAG DAY (US)**	15
19 **JUNETEENTH (US)**	20 ○ **SUMMER SOLSTICE**	21	22
26	27 ◐	28	29

KNIGHT

OF SWORDS

You are an ambitious thinker and are driven to succeed. You have a high intellect and you apply that to your decision making. Confident in what you believe, you charge forward with conviction but don't forget to stop and think. Be certain about your course of action. Are you truly doing the right thing, or acting on old impulses? Look before you leap.

MAY/JUNE

MONDAY (MAY) SPRING BANK HOLIDAY (UK) / MEMORIAL DAY (US)

27

TUESDAY (MAY)

28

WEDNESDAY (MAY)

29

THURSDAY (MAY) ◗

30

FRIDAY (MAY)

31

SATURDAY FIRST DAY OF PRIDE MONTH

1

SUNDAY

2

JUNE 2024

MONDAY

3

TUESDAY

4

WEDNESDAY

5

THURSDAY ●

6

FRIDAY

7

SATURDAY

8

SUNDAY

9

THE DEVIL

Go deep inside to get to know your subconscious self, the one some call their shadow. What do you truly want or crave? Have there been times when those desires overwhelmed you?

JUNE 2024

MONDAY

10

TUESDAY

11

WEDNESDAY

12

THURSDAY

13

FRIDAY FLAG DAY (US) 🌙

14

SATURDAY

15

SUNDAY FATHER'S DAY (US / CAN / UK)

16

TEN OF WANDS

You might have been taking on too much.
This is a time to think about what you want to
accomplish, the effort it takes, and whether
you should ask for help.

JUNE 2024

MONDAY

17

TUESDAY

18

WEDNESDAY JUNETEENTH (US)

19

THURSDAY SUMMER SOLSTICE

20

FRIDAY ○   21

SATURDAY   22

SUNDAY   23

KING OF PENTACLES
Your self-discipline is paying off and rewards
are on their way. Expect success in business,
leadership, and finances.

JUNE 2024

MONDAY   24

TUESDAY   25

WEDNESDAY   26

THURSDAY   27

FRIDAY 🌓

28

SATURDAY

29

SUNDAY

30

TAROT TIP

Reading the cards is a skill that you learn over
time. Be patient with yourself. The learning
never stops.

JULY

THE HERMIT

THE
HERMIT

This is a time to draw your attention inward and dig deep within. This is an opportunity for reflection and serenity, so try not to go through it being critical of yourself. Let go of the unnecessary demands on your psyche (stop scrolling!) and make space for yourself. Even the moon has a dormant period for introspection and rest. Enjoy your own company.

LAY OUT A THREE-CARD SPREAD AND ASK THE CARDS

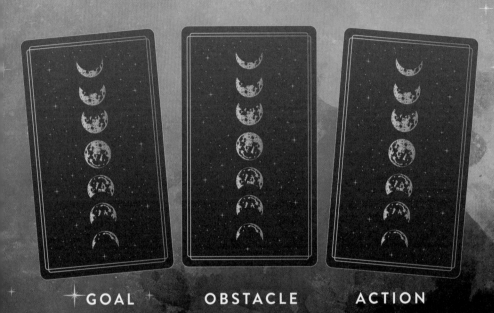

GOAL · OBSTACLE · ACTION

1. What goal do I need to focus on this month?

....

2. What obstacle or challenge will I face this month?

....

3. In what ways can I limit unnecessary distractions?

....

JULY 2024

NOTES	SUNDAY	MONDAY	TUESDAY
		1	2
		CANADA DAY (CAN)	
	7	8	9
	14	15	16
○	21	22	23
	28	29	30

JULY 2024

WEDNESDAY	THURSDAY	FRIDAY	SATURDAY
3	4 ●	5	6
	INDEPENDENCE DAY (US)		
10	11	12 ◖	13
17	18	19	20
24	25	26 ◗	27
31			

FOUR

OF WANDS

You have been on a journey and undergone significant change. It could be time for you to rest and recuperate. Find your place of refuge. Consider how far you have come.

JULY

MONDAY CANADA DAY (CAN)

1

TUESDAY

2

WEDNESDAY

3

THURSDAY INDEPENDENCE DAY (US)

4

FRIDAY ●

5

SATURDAY

6

SUNDAY

7

JULY 2024

MONDAY
8

TUESDAY
9

WEDNESDAY
10

THURSDAY
11

FRIDAY

12

SATURDAY

13

SUNDAY

14

SIX OF WANDS

Things are not perfect but you have been able to marshal your skills and meet your goal. This could be a time to chill out and bask in your success.

MONDAY

15

TUESDAY

16

WEDNESDAY

17

THURSDAY

18

FRIDAY

19

SATURDAY

20

SUNDAY ○

21

ACE OF PENTACLES

A new opportunity has presented itself. This might be your chance to achieve what you have been striving for. Are you willing to do what needs to be done?

JULY 2024

MONDAY

22

TUESDAY

23

WEDNESDAY

24

THURSDAY

25

FRIDAY

26

SATURDAY

27

SUNDAY

28

TAROT TIP

Manage your expectations. You can't force
the cards to tell you what you want to hear,
so approach a reading with a clean slate.

AUGUST

THE HIEROPHANT

THE
HIEROPHANT

You could be on the verge of attaining knowledge, wisdom, or a blessing. You have a sense of permanence but also mystery. You may want to go looking for advice. Seeking deeper knowledge is strongly advised. What do you have yet to learn? What is it that you want to know? Who is it you can turn to? Don't hold yourself back from seeking counsel and clarity.

LAY OUT A THREE-CARD SPREAD AND ASK THE CARDS

GOAL   OBSTACLE   ACTION

1. What goal do I need to focus on this month?

....

2. What obstacle or challenge will I face this month?

....

3. What deeper knowledge do I need to help me reach my goals?

....

AUGUST 2024

NOTES	SUNDAY	MONDAY	TUESDAY
	● 4	5	6
		SUMMER BANK HOLIDAY (UK-SCT)	
	11 ◐	12	13
	18 ○	19	20
	25 ◑	26	27
		SUMMER BANK HOLIDAY (UK-ENG / NIR / WAL)	

AUGUST 2024

WEDNESDAY	THURSDAY	FRIDAY	SATURDAY
	1	2	3
7	8	9	10
14	15	16	17
21	22	23	24
28	29	30	31

EIGHT

OF PENTACLES

You have skills, no doubt. You've worked hard but consider yourself still an apprentice. Be dedicated, serious, and sincere. Continue to put your all into what you do. Give yourself a chance to move from apprentice to master by honing your skills. Practice makes perfect!

MONDAY (JULY)

29

TUESDAY (JULY)

30

WEDNESDAY (JULY)

31

THURSDAY

1

FRIDAY

2

SATURDAY

3

SUNDAY ●

4

AUGUST 2024

MONDAY SUMMER BANK HOLIDAY (UK-SCT)

5

TUESDAY

6

WEDNESDAY

7

THURSDAY

8

FRIDAY

9

SATURDAY

10

SUNDAY

11

PAGE OF PENTACLES

There is much for you to learn.
Contemplation is your solace. Some might
think you are daydreaming, but in fact you
are planning and growing.

AUGUST 2024

MONDAY ◖

12

TUESDAY

13

WEDNESDAY

14

THURSDAY

15

FRIDAY

16

SATURDAY

17

SUNDAY

18

FOUR OF CUPS

New opportunities are abundant right
now. Be discerning on what's important to
you and decline projects that don't align
with your dreams.

AUGUST 2024

MONDAY ○   19

TUESDAY   20

WEDNESDAY   21

THURSDAY   22

FRIDAY 23

SATURDAY 24

SUNDAY 25

TAROT TIP

If you're in a pinch and need quick advice,
draw a single card. Ask how you can
approach the situation in the best way
possible for everyone involved.

SEPTEMBER

THE EMPEROR

THE EMPEROR

Consider stability, power, and logic. Take charge and embrace this chance to set healthy boundaries, bring order to chaos, and put your potential into action. Inhabit your confidence fully and do not apologize for who you are. You are in charge of your life, so sit tall on your throne.

LAY OUT A THREE-CARD SPREAD AND ASK THE CARDS

GOAL **OBSTACLE** **ACTION**

1. What goal do I need to focus on this month?

....

....

2. What obstacle or challenge will I face this month?

....

....

3. In what ways can I bring order to my life?

....

....

SEPTEMBER 2024

NOTES	SUNDAY	MONDAY	TUESDAY
....	1 ●	2	3
....			
....		LABOR DAY (US)	
....	FATHER'S DAY (AUS / NZ)	LABOUR DAY (CAN)	
....	8	9	10
....			
....			
....	GRANDPARENTS' DAY (US)		
....	15	16 ○	17
....			
....	FIRST DAY OF NATIONAL HISPANIC HERITAGE MONTH		
....	22	23 ☽	24
....			
....			
....	FALL EQUINOX		
....	29	30	
....			

SEPTEMBER 2024

WEDNESDAY	THURSDAY	FRIDAY	SATURDAY
4	5	6	7
11 PATRIOT DAY (US)	12	13	14
18	19	20	21
25	26	27	28

SEVEN

OF CUPS

Choices! So many choices. But not all are created equal. Maybe money, power, or fame sound enticing, but choose your path wisely. Not everything is what it's cracked up to be. Look closely. Take your time. Try to see clearly. Dig deep for the truth. Discern between wishful thinking and reality.

AUGUST/SEPTEMBER

MONDAY (AUGUST) SUMMER BANK HOLIDAY (UK-ENG / NIR / WAL)

26

TUESDAY (AUGUST)

27

WEDNESDAY (AUGUST)

28

THURSDAY (AUGUST)

29

FRIDAY (AUGUST)

30

SATURDAY (AUGUST)

31

SUNDAY FATHER'S DAY (AUS / NZ)

1

SEPTEMBER 2024

MONDAY LABOR DAY (US) / LABOUR DAY (CAN) ●

2

TUESDAY

3

WEDNESDAY

4

THURSDAY

5

FRIDAY

6

SATURDAY

7

SUNDAY GRANDPARENTS' DAY (US)

8

EIGHT OF CUPS

Not every victory is easily earned. There are
setbacks in your journey. These can be cause
for concern or a reason to recoup. Give
yourself more chances. Do not be afraid to ask
for direction.

SEPTEMBER 2024

MONDAY

9

TUESDAY

10

WEDNESDAY PATRIOT DAY (US)

11

THURSDAY

12

FRIDAY 13

SATURDAY 14

SUNDAY FIRST DAY OF NATIONAL HISPANIC HERITAGE MONTH 15

FIVE OF SWORDS

Confidence is ascendant in the aftermath of a
victorious outcome. But things are not always
that simple. Remember to be humble and a
gracious winner.

SEPTEMBER 2024

MONDAY

16

TUESDAY ◯

17

WEDNESDAY

18

THURSDAY

19

FRIDAY   20

SATURDAY   21

SUNDAY FALL EQUINOX   22

QUEEN OF PENTACLES

Nurturing is hard work! Are you taking
care of others or are you too busy
taking care of yourself? Maybe things
need rebalancing. Security can come at
a price but it is usually worth it.

SEPTEMBER 2024

MONDAY 23

TUESDAY ◗ 24

WEDNESDAY 25

THURSDAY 26

FRIDAY

27

SATURDAY

28

SUNDAY

29

TAROT TIP

Before doing a reading for someone else, take
care to not let your own questions invade by
asking them to be clear on their intentions for
the reading. You must be in sync.

OCTOBER

THE CHARIOT

THE
CHARIOT

You are persevering against difficult odds. A significant detour is coming but you are equipped to face it head on. Now is not the time to be passive. Tap into your sense of perseverance, awaken your strong will, and don't let anything derail you from your path. Keep your focus and remain confident in your abilities.

LAY OUT A THREE-CARD SPREAD AND ASK THE CARDS

GOAL   OBSTACLE   ACTION

1. What goal do I need to focus on this month?

....

2. What obstacle or challenge will I face this month?

....

3. Even when my life goes in unplanned ways, how can I adjust and keep my eyes on my goal?

....

OCTOBER 2024

NOTES	SUNDAY	MONDAY	TUESDAY
			1
	6	7	8
		LABOUR DAY (AUS-ACT / NSW / SA)	
	13	14	15
		INDIGENOUS PEOPLES' DAY (US) COLUMBUS DAY (US) THANKSGIVING DAY (CAN)	
	20	21	22
	27	28	29
		LABOUR DAY (NZ)	

OCTOBER 2024

WEDNESDAY	THURSDAY	FRIDAY	SATURDAY
● 2	3	4	5
ROSH HASHANAH (BEGINS AT SUNDOWN)			
9	☽ 10	11	12
		YOM KIPPUR (BEGINS AT SUNDOWN)	
16 ○	17	18	19
SUKKOT (BEGINS AT SUNDOWN)			
23 ☾	24	25	26
	SIMCHAT TORAH (BEGINS AT SUNDOWN)		
30	31		
	FIRST DAY OF DIWALI **HALLOWEEN**		

FOUR

OF SWORDS

Y ou have gone through some considerable challenges, beaten the odds, and now it's time for a rest. Take time to tune the world out, put down the pressures, and go with your own flow. Resting is the best way to recharge so that you can be your very best self. Pat yourself on the back and relax.

SEPTEMBER/OCTOBER

MONDAY (SEPTEMBER)

30

TUESDAY

1

WEDNESDAY ROSH HASHANAH (BEGINS AT SUNDOWN) ●

2

THURSDAY

3

FRIDAY

4

SATURDAY

5

SUNDAY

6

OCTOBER 2024

MONDAY LABOUR DAY (AUS-ACT / NSW / SA)

7

TUESDAY

8

WEDNESDAY

9

THURSDAY

10

FRIDAY YOM KIPPUR (BEGINS AT SUNDOWN)

11

SATURDAY

12

SUNDAY

13

THREE OF SWORDS

Loss and pain are unavoidable. They are also
not permanent. Do not avoid what happened
to you. Facing your hurt can bring it down to
size and make it easier to cope with.

OCTOBER 2024

MONDAY INDIGENOUS PEOPLES' DAY (US) / COLUMBUS DAY (US) / THANKSGIVING DAY (CAN)

14

TUESDAY

15

WEDNESDAY SUKKOT (BEGINS AT SUNDOWN)

16

THURSDAY ○

17

FRIDAY 18

SATURDAY 19

SUNDAY 20

KING OF WANDS

There is a leader within you. When you point the way, others trust and follow. But what is your vision? Be clear on your goals. Make a plan and be a success.

OCTOBER 2024

MONDAY

21

TUESDAY

22

WEDNESDAY

23

THURSDAY SIMCHAT TORAH (BEGINS AT SUNDOWN) ◗

24

FRIDAY 25

SATURDAY 26

SUNDAY 27

TAROT TIP
To sync up with a person you're reading for,
try taking three deep breaths together or do a
short meditation in sync.

NOVEMBER

THE MOON

THE
MOON

Your fears and illusions are fighting for front-row seats and you might be projecting these into your present and future. Let go of the pain of past experiences and face the day with courage. Release fears and misconceptions that haunt you. Familiar perceptions aren't always healthy, even though they feel safe at time. Let go and make room for hope.

LAY OUT A THREE-CARD SPREAD AND ASK THE CARDS

GOAL   OBSTACLE   ACTION

1. What goal do I need to focus on this month?

....

2. What obstacle or challenge will I face this month?

....

3. What have I been holding on to that would be healthy to release?

....

NOVEMBER 2024

NOTES	SUNDAY	MONDAY	TUESDAY
	3	4	5
			ELECTION DAY (US)
	10	11	12
		VETERANS DAY (US)	
	17	18	19
	24	25	26

NOVEMBER 2024

WEDNESDAY	THURSDAY	FRIDAY	SATURDAY
		● 1	2
		ALL SAINTS' DAY	
6	7	8 ◗	9
13	14 ○	15	16
20	21 ◖	22	23
27	28	29	30
	THANKSGIVING DAY (US)	NATIVE AMERICAN HERITAGE DAY (US)	

QUEEN

OF WANDS

Your confidence is an asset, as is your luck. Charm, magnetism, and optimism bring others into your orbit. Embody creativity, spark passion, and listen to your nurturing side. This is a good time to focus on your spiritual aspects and manifest your dreams.

OCTOBER/NOVEMBER

MONDAY (OCTOBER) LABOUR DAY (NZ)

28

TUESDAY (OCTOBER)

29

WEDNESDAY (OCTOBER)

30

THURSDAY (OCTOBER) FIRST DAY OF DIWALI / HALLOWEEN

31

FRIDAY ALL SAINTS' DAY ●

1

SATURDAY

2

SUNDAY

3

NOVEMBER 2024

MONDAY

4

TUESDAY ELECTION DAY (US)

5

WEDNESDAY

6

THURSDAY

7

FRIDAY 8

SATURDAY ◗ 9

SUNDAY 10

JUDGEMENT

Actions have consequences, even if
they are not always apparent at first.
Have you been hurt? Have you been the
hurter? Examine the past and determine
how you will right the wrongs.

NOVEMBER 2024

MONDAY VETERANS DAY (US)

11

TUESDAY

12

WEDNESDAY

13

THURSDAY

14

FRIDAY ◯

15

SATURDAY

16

SUNDAY

17

NINE OF PENTACLES

Prosperity and achievement might be in your
grasp. You have something to celebrate. Are
you solitary in this state or is it a party? Learn
to luxuriate.

NOVEMBER 2024

MONDAY

18

TUESDAY

19

WEDNESDAY

20

THURSDAY

21

FRIDAY

22

SATURDAY

23

SUNDAY

24

TAROT TIP

If the answer to your question is not coming through, it could mean that the answer is unclear or unknowable at that time. Try reframing your question to be more broad.

DECEMBER

THE HIGH PRIESTESS

THE
HIGH PRIESTESS

You have intuition, also known as an inner voice. Sometimes it can be hard to hear. Tune out the world! Calm things down and open yourself to what your deeper, subconscious self is trying to say. Embrace the mystery of your life and trust your instincts.

LAY OUT A THREE-CARD SPREAD AND ASK THE CARDS

GOAL   OBSTACLE   ACTION

1. What goal do I need to focus on this month?

....

2. What obstacle or challenge will I face this month?

....

3. In what ways can I listen to my inner voice and allow my intuition to guide me?

....

DECEMBER 2024

NOTES	SUNDAY	MONDAY	TUESDAY
	● 1	2	3
			INTERNATIONAL DAY OF PERSONS WITH DISABILITIES
	WORLD AIDS DAY		
	◑ 8	9	10
			HUMAN RIGHTS DAY
	○ 15	16	17
	◗ 22	23	24
			CHRISTMAS EVE
	29 ● 30		31
			NEW YEAR'S EVE

DECEMBER 2024

WEDNESDAY	THURSDAY	FRIDAY	SATURDAY
4	5	6	7
11	12	13	14
18	19	20	21 WINTER SOLSTICE
25 CHRISTMAS DAY HANUKKAH (BEGINS AT SUNDOWN)	26 BOXING DAY (UK / CAN / AUS / NZ) FIRST DAY OF KWANZAA	27	28

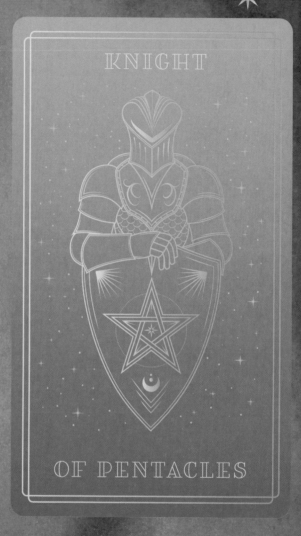

KNIGHT

OF PENTACLES

All work and no play may not sound practical, but it can be satisfying. You are steady and responsible. Predictable? Sometimes. But predictability brings trust and confidence. Do not forget that your efforts have a purpose and the work you're doing gets you closer to your goals every day.

NOVEMBER/DECEMBER

MONDAY (NOVEMBER)

25

TUESDAY (NOVEMBER)

26

WEDNESDAY (NOVEMBER)

27

THURSDAY (NOVEMBER) THANKSGIVING DAY (US)

28

FRIDAY (NOVEMBER) NATIVE AMERICAN HERITAGE DAY (US)

29

SATURDAY (NOVEMBER)

30

SUNDAY WORLD AIDS DAY ●

1

DECEMBER 2024

MONDAY

2

TUESDAY INTERNATIONAL DAY OF PERSONS WITH DISABILITIES

3

WEDNESDAY

4

THURSDAY

5

FRIDAY 6

SATURDAY 7

SUNDAY 8

SEVEN OF WANDS

You have already come a long way but are
feeling somewhat alone in your struggle. The
odds might be out of focus, but they are
ultimately in your favor.

DECEMBER 2024

MONDAY

9

TUESDAY **HUMAN RIGHTS DAY**

10

WEDNESDAY

11

THURSDAY

12

FRIDAY 13

SATURDAY 14

SUNDAY ○ 15

TEN OF CUPS

You might not have everything you want
but you likely have everything you need.
Think about what truly matters. Focus
on the gifts that money can't buy.

DECEMBER 2024

MONDAY

16

TUESDAY

17

WEDNESDAY

18

THURSDAY

19

FRIDAY

20

SATURDAY WINTER SOLSTICE

21

SUNDAY ☽

22

KING OF SWORDS

Listen to your inner voice and tap into your
wisdom. Find ways to incorporate these into
your life to benefit yourself and others.

DECEMBER 2024

MONDAY

23

TUESDAY CHRISTMAS EVE

24

WEDNESDAY CHRISTMAS DAY / HANUKKAH (BEGINS AT SUNDOWN)

25

THURSDAY BOXING DAY (UK / CAN / AUS / NZ) / FIRST DAY OF KWANZAA

26

FRIDAY 27

SATURDAY 28

SUNDAY 29

TAROT TIP

When learning to interpret messages, read more than one book. The more information you have from different perspectives, the better understanding you'll gain.

DECEMBER 2024

MONDAY ●

30

TUESDAY NEW YEAR'S EVE

31

WEDNESDAY (JANUARY) NEW YEAR'S DAY

1

TUESDAY (JANUARY)

2

NOTES

NOTES

Brimming with creative inspiration, how-to projects, and useful information to enrich your everyday life, quarto.com is a favorite destination for those pursuing their interests and passions.

© 2023 by Quarto Publishing Group USA Inc.

First published in 2023 by Rock Point,
an imprint of The Quarto Group
142 West 36th Street, 4th Floor
New York, NY 10018, USA
T (212) 779-4972 F (212) 779-6058
www.Quarto.com

Rock Point titles are also available at discount for retail, wholesale, promotional, and bulk purchase.
For details, contact the Special Sales Manager by email at specialsales@quarto.com
or by mail at The Quarto Group, Attn: Special Sales Manager,
100 Cummings Center Suite 265D, Beverly, MA 01915 USA.

10 9 8 7 6 5 4 3 2 1

ISBN: 978-1-63106-953-6

Publisher: Rage Kindelsperger
Creative Director: Laura Drew
Managing Editor: Cara Donaldson
Editor: Sara Bonacum
Cover Design: Laura Drew
Text: Chris Barsanti
Interior Layout: B. Middleworth

Printed in China

This book provides general information on tarot and positive spiritual habits. However, it should not be relied upon as recommending or promoting any specific diagnosis or method of treatment for a particular condition, and it is not intended as a substitute for medical advice or for direct diagnosis and treatment of a medical condition by a qualified physician. Readers who have questions about a particular condition, possible treatments for that condition, or possible reactions from the condition or its treatment should consult a physician or other qualified healthcare professional.

All moon phases shown are for the Eastern Time Zone.